Be A
Pet Expert

BE A RABBIT EXPERT

By Gemma Barder

CRABTREE
PUBLISHING COMPANY
WWW.CRABTREEBOOKS.COM

BE A RABBIT EXPERT

With their twitchy noses and long, soft ears, it's no wonder rabbits are one of the world's most popular pets. Rabbits are great company and fun to look after, but there are a lot of things you need to know before becoming a real pet expert! In this book you'll discover different breeds of rabbits, where the first pet rabbits came from, and the best way to care for your bunny. When you've finished reading, there's an exciting quiz to reveal if you've really become a pet expert!

CRABTREE
PUBLISHING COMPANY
WWW.CRABTREEBOOKS.COM

Published in Canada
Crabtree Publishing
616 Welland Avenue
St. Catharines, ON
L2M 5V6

Published in the United States
Crabtree Publishing
347 Fifth Ave,
Suite 1402-145
New York, NY 10016

Published in 2021 by CRABTREE PUBLISHING COMPANY.

First published in 2019 by Wayland
Copyright © Hodder and Stoughton, 2019

Author: Gemma Barder

Editorial director: Kathy Middleton

Editors: Dynamo Limited, Robin Johnson

Cover and interior design: Dynamo Limited

Proofreader: Melissa Boyce

**Production coordinator
& Prepress technician:** Samara Parent

Print coordinator: Katherine Berti

Printed in the U.S.A./072020/CG20200429

Photographs
(l - left, r - right, br - bottom right, bc - bottom center, cl - center left, tr - top right)

All images courtesy of Getty Images iStock except:
Stefan Petru Andronache/Shuttertstock: front cover and title page r; Denis Tabler/Shutterstock: front cover and title page l; Claudio Contreras/Naturepl.com: 7b, 29tr, 30; Michael Andersen/Alamy: 3tr, 5br; imageBROKER/Alamy: 16; Keren Su/China Span/Alamy: 18bc; Beryl Peters Collection/Alamy: 19bc; Trinity Mirror / Mirrorpix/Alamy: 19tr; CuriousCatPhotos/Alamy: 20br

Every attempt has been made to clear copyright. Should there be any inadvertent omission, please apply to the publisher for rectification.

Library and Archives Canada Cataloguing in Publication

Title: Be a rabbit expert / by Gemma Barder.
Other titles: Rabbits
Names: Barder, Gemma, author.
Description: Series statement: Be a pet expert |
  Previously published under title: Rabbits. | Includes index.
Identifiers: Canadiana (print) 20200222708 |
  Canadiana (ebook) 20200222740 |
  ISBN 9780778780199 (hardcover) |
  ISBN 9780778780472 (softcover) |
  ISBN 9781427125613 (HTML)
Subjects: LCSH: Rabbits—Juvenile literature. |
  LCSH: Rabbit breeds—Juvenile literature.
Classification: LCC SF453.2 .B37 2021 | DDC j636.932/2—dc23

Library of Congress Cataloging-in-Publication Data

Names: Barder, Gemma, author.
Title: Be a rabbit expert / by Gemma Barder.
Description: New York : Crabtree Publishing Company, 2021. |
  Series: Be a pet expert | Includes index.
Identifiers: LCCN 2020015990 (print) | LCCN 2020015991 (ebook) |
  ISBN 9780778780199 (hardcover) |
  ISBN 9780778780472 (paperback) |
  ISBN 9781427125613 (ebook)
Subjects: LCSH: Rabbits--Juvenile literature.
Classification: LCC SF453.2 .B365 2021 (print) | LCC SF453.2 (ebook) |
  DDC 632/.6932--dc23
LC record available at https://lccn.loc.gov/2020015990
LC ebook record available at https://lccn.loc.gov/2020015991

CONTENTS

BUNNY BANTER

FIVE FACTS

BUNNY BONANZA

From floppy ears to magnificent markings, get to know these popular bunny **breeds** a bit better.

HOLLAND LOP

This floppy-eared bunny has been popular since the 1950s. With its long ears, beautiful **coat**, and friendly personality, Holland **Lops** make perfect pets. They don't like to be kept cooped up in a **hutch**, though, so make sure you give them plenty of exercise.

MINI REX

The Mini Rex rabbit has a thick coat, straight, soft ears, and a calm personality—which makes it the perfect pet rabbit! Mini Rex rabbits come in many different colors and markings and are slightly smaller than other **domesticated** breeds.

14 million

40 million

There are an estimated 14 million pet rabbits in the world, and scientists believe there could be nearly 40 million in the wild!

DUTCH RABBIT

You can easily spot Dutch rabbits by their distinctive color patterns. Despite their name, they were actually developed in the United Kingdom and were the most popular breed of rabbit for a long time before smaller breeds were introduced. They make smart and playful pets.

JERSEY WOOLY

As their name suggests, these little bunnies have soft coats that feel like wool. They need to be brushed at least once a week. These small rabbits have straight ears and compact bodies. Jersey Woolys are often known as "no-kick bunnies" because they don't usually kick or bite.

DID YOU KNOW?

A female rabbit is called a doe, and a male rabbit is called a buck.

RARE RABBITS

From the smallest to the most mysterious, take a look at these super-rare rabbits.

COLUMBIA BASIN PYGMY RABBIT

These tiny bunnies are the world's smallest breed of rabbit. They weigh only around 1 pound (0.45 kg) when fully grown and are about the same size as a kitten! In the wild, they live in a small area of Washington state and were almost **extinct** in the 1990s.

SOUTHEAST ASIAN STRIPED RABBIT

This unusual rabbit was discovered 20 years ago in the remote Annamite Mountains of Laos and Vietnam, and sightings have been rare ever since. Its fur is light brown with dark-brown stripes. It has short ears and can grow to around 16 inches (40 cm) long. But there is still much more to learn about this mysterious bunny!

TEDDYWIDDER

Is that a rabbit or a big pom-pom? Teddywidders come from the Netherlands, Germany, and Belgium and have fur that grows more than 2 inches (5 cm) long. Teddywidders have floppy (or lop) ears, which makes them slightly different than their Teddy Dwerg cousins that have pointy ears.

DID YOU KNOW?

The volcano rabbit lets out a high-pitched squeak when it thinks it is in danger, rather than thumping its feet on the ground like other breeds do.

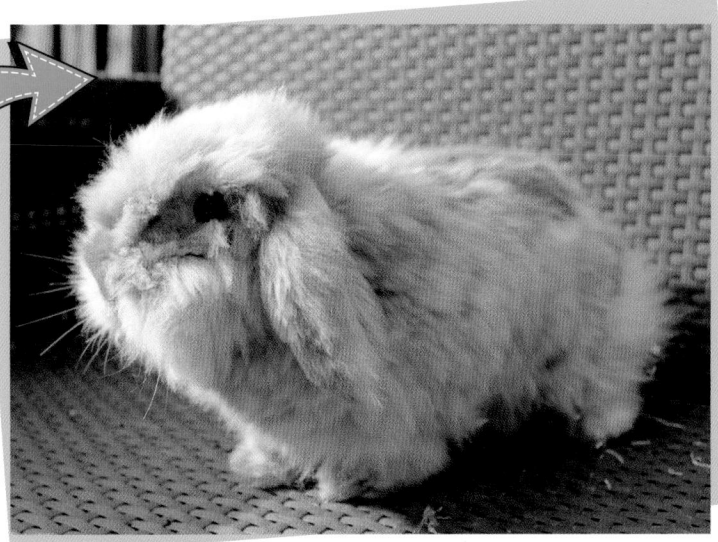

VOLCANO RABBIT

Volcano rabbits live in mountainous areas of Mexico. They are very hard to spot and in some areas have been declared extinct. The destruction of their natural habitat, together with **climate change**, has forced this bunny breed to make its home higher up the mountains. Volcano rabbits are the second-smallest rabbit breed in the world and have short, fluffy ears.

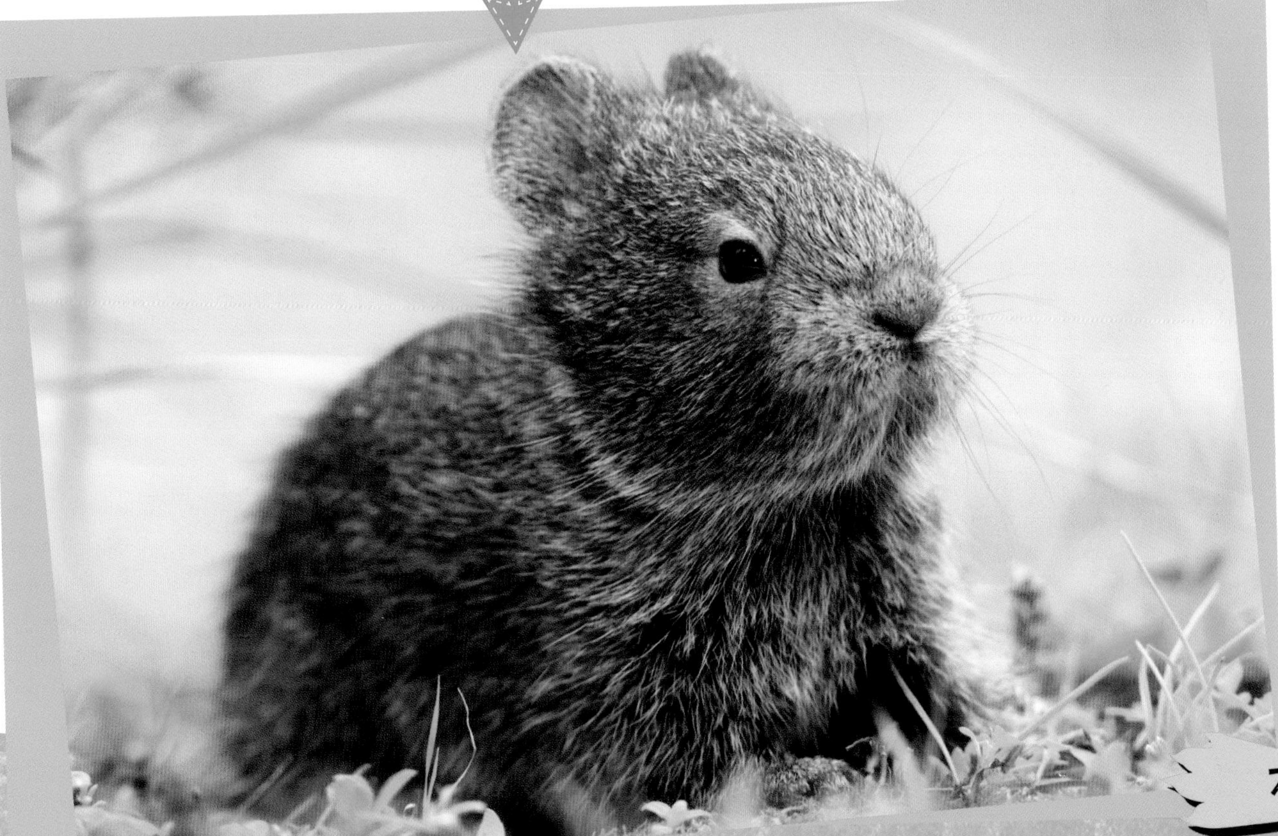

BUNNY BANTER

Rabbits have a secret language to tell you (and other rabbits) how they are feeling. Find out exactly what it means when your bunny hops, thumps, and twitches.

EARS

Different rabbit breeds have different types of ears (straight, floppy, small), so it can be hard to tell what they are doing with them. A little shake of the ears followed by jumping shows playfulness and excitement. Ears perked up mean rabbits are feeling cautious about what is going on around them.

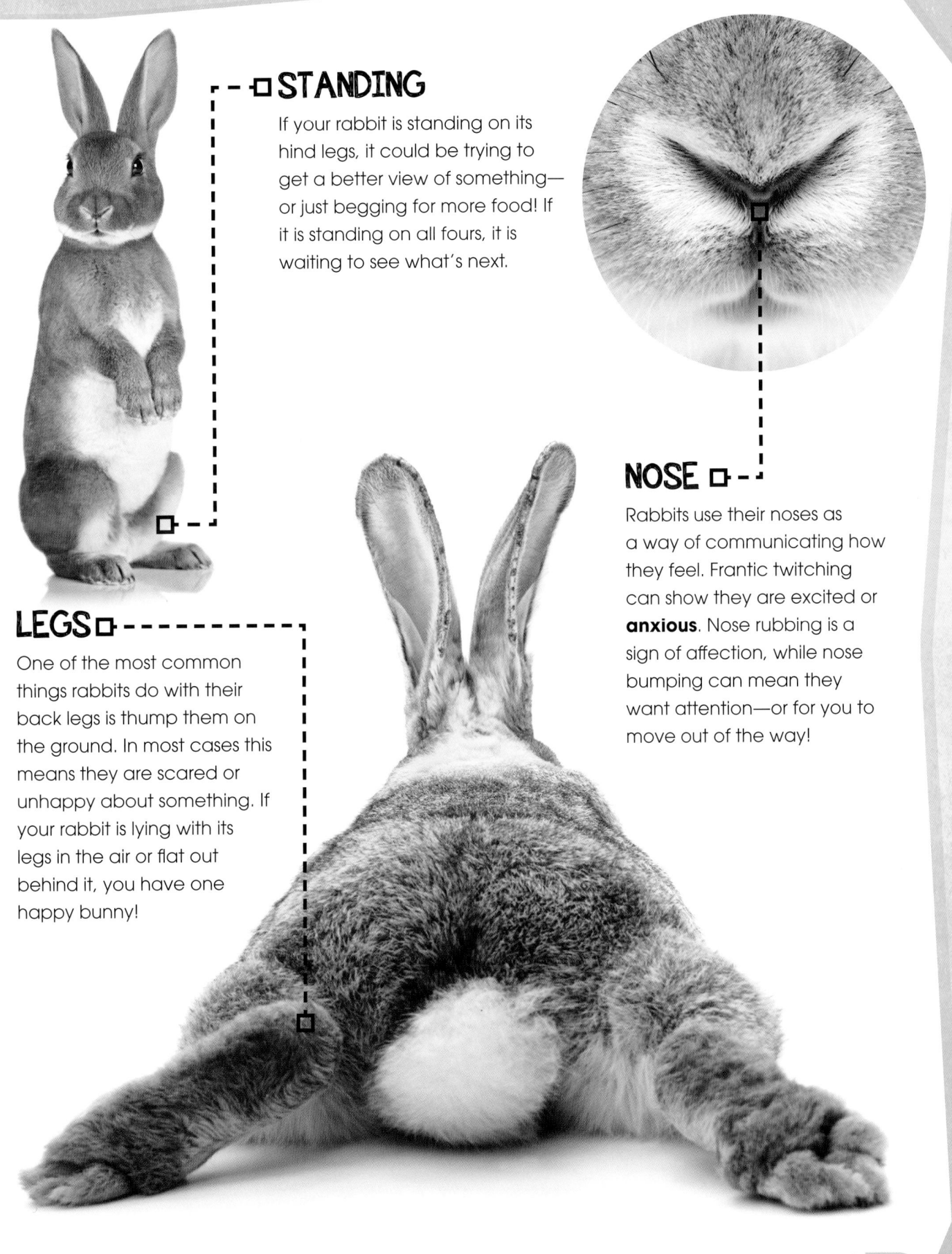

STANDING

If your rabbit is standing on its hind legs, it could be trying to get a better view of something—or just begging for more food! If it is standing on all fours, it is waiting to see what's next.

NOSE

Rabbits use their noses as a way of communicating how they feel. Frantic twitching can show they are excited or **anxious**. Nose rubbing is a sign of affection, while nose bumping can mean they want attention—or for you to move out of the way!

LEGS

One of the most common things rabbits do with their back legs is thump them on the ground. In most cases this means they are scared or unhappy about something. If your rabbit is lying with its legs in the air or flat out behind it, you have one happy bunny!

KITTENS

These cute little bundles don't take long to grow up! Read all about baby bunnies—called kittens—before they hop away!

EARLY DAYS

Kittens are blind and furless when they are born. They live snuggled up to their brothers and sisters in fur-lined nests until they can see and their fur grows. Unlike birds, mother rabbits don't sit on their nests and will leave the kittens for long periods of time.

DID YOU KNOW?

The average number of kittens in a litter is eight to nine. The world record for kittens in one litter is 24!

TIME TO GROW

A baby rabbit should stay with its mother until it is at least eight weeks old. Kittens become adult rabbits when they are around six months old, which is when they can start to have kittens of their own.

WEANING

Newborn kittens drink only their mother's milk. After two weeks, they start to eat other foods such as hay and carrots, before moving on to a variety of other foods.

30 days **660 days**

Rabbits are pregnant for only 30 days, while elephants can be pregnant for 660 days!

BUNNY LOVE!

Discover everything you need to know about keeping your bunny happy, healthy, and well fed!

FOOD AND DRINK

Rabbits need a supply of fresh hay at all times. Bunnies like to **graze** rather than eating a lot of food at once, so snacking between meals is definitely OK! They like fresh vegetables and rabbit pellets, which give them plenty of fiber. They also need fresh water throughout the day in a bowl or bottle.

GROOMING

Rabbits like to keep themselves clean, but that doesn't mean you can leave them to look after themselves completely. Long-haired rabbits need to be brushed at least once a week to keep their fur from **matting**, and all rabbits need their nails trimmed regularly.

FUN WITH FRIENDS

A happy rabbit is a rabbit with friends. Rabbits need to be kept with at least one other bunny, and they like to see you too! Spend time with your rabbit at least twice a day.

HEATSTROKE

If your bunny is outside on a hot day, watch for signs of **heatstroke**, which include red ears, drooling, moving slowly, and sometimes **convulsions**.

BUNNY PROOFING

If you are planning to exercise your rabbit indoors, you'll need to do some bunny proofing first! Make sure all wires are tied up out of reach or covered in plastic tubes. Put plastic guards on your baseboards too.

HEALTH

Bunnies can get sick, so it is a good idea to keep an eye on how they behave. If your rabbit is eating less or having trouble pooping, it could be a sign of illness. Watch for an extra-scratchy bunny because it could have fleas!

PLAYTIME

When you play with your rabbit, come down to its level and play on the floor because rabbits don't like to be high up. Make a castle out of old cardboard boxes for your rabbit to explore and chew.

DID YOU KNOW?

Rabbits and guinea pigs do not get along! They don't understand each other and can get into fights.

FACT FILE

TOYS!

Rabbits love to play with toys like these:

- cardboard tubes stuffed with hay
- baby toys (not electronic)
- tunnels

RABBIT RULES

Here are some tips on the dos and don'ts of bunny care.

DO:

Keep rabbits in pairs or in threes because they love company. ✔

Provide two bowls or bottles of water if you are away for more than a few hours. ✔

Buy good-quality food and hay. ✔

Get your bunnies vaccinated. **Your** vet **will tell you which vaccinations they need.** ✔

Research the right type of rabbit for you. ✔

Brush your bunnies regularly. ✔

Keep vegetable peelings to add to their diet. ✔

Play with them often. ✔

DON'T:

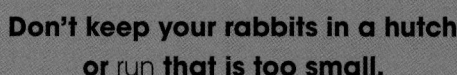

Don't keep your rabbits in a hutch or run that is too small.

Don't keep them outside when it is very cold.

Don't pet or play with your bunnies when they are anxious. Leave them alone to calm down.

Don't keep them in a cage with a wire floor because it is bad for their feet.

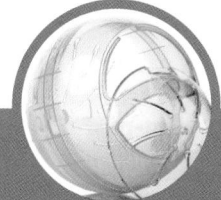

Don't give them toys they could get stuck in, such as a hamster ball.

Don't forget to clean out their hutch regularly.

FOOD FOR RABBITS

 basil
 celery
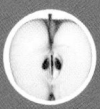 apple seeds
 chocolate

 bok choy
 clover
 avocado
 fried food

 carrot tops
 coriander
 bread
 onion

RABBIT HABITAT

There's a lot to consider when you begin to create the perfect palace for your rabbit friends. Get started by reading these hints and tips.

INDOORS OR OUTDOORS?

It can be confusing to decide whether your rabbits should live indoors or outdoors. Before you bring your bunnies home, talk to the breeder to see how they have been living. Also consider talking to your vet. Always remember to bring your rabbits indoors if the weather is very cold or hot.

FACT FILE

The Be a Pet Expert guide to hutch size:
- It should be tall enough for your adult-sized bunny to sit up straight on its back legs.
- It should be wide enough for your adult-sized bunny to hop twice.
- It should be long enough for your adult-sized bunny to hop three times.
- Attach a run to your hutch so your bunny gets plenty of exercise.

HAPPIEST HUTCH

A hutch should have a place for sleeping and a place for looking out. Most hutches have a dark area as well as a section covered in mesh or wire for your bunny to look through.

DID YOU KNOW?

Any plant that is grown from a bulb is toxic to rabbits. This includes daffodils and tulips!

GETTING READY

Before you introduce your rabbit to its new home, it's time to make it nice and cozy! Start by lining the bottom of the cage with newspaper, then top that with wood shavings (but not cedar or pine because these can be **toxic**). Line the sleeping area of the hutch with soft hay too.

FACT FILE

Where to place your outdoor hutch:

- **C**hoose a spot that is close to the house.
- A shady spot is a great choice for warmer weather.
- Be aware of any plants that might hang over the hutch and make sure they aren't toxic to hungry bunnies.
- Make sure the hutch is away from other animals.

DID YOU KNOW?

You should clean out your rabbit's hutch once a week. Use only pet-safe cleaning products.

THE HISTORY OF RABBITS

From the Spanish wilderness to your backyard, bunnies have a very interesting history.

ROMANS

The ancient Romans knew how important rabbits were for providing food to eat and warm clothing to wear. Although the Romans built rabbit farms, the rabbits were famous for tunneling to freedom.

300 B.C.E.

220 B.C.E.

40 C.E.

LAND OF THE RABBITS!

One theory about how Spain got its name dates back to around 2,300 years ago. The theory goes that the ancient Romans called it "Hispania," a word that came from another ancient language and means "Land of the Rabbits."

ACROSS THE OCEANS

As the ancient Romans traveled across the globe, so did their rabbits! Romans would take the rabbits on voyages for food and breed them in each new country they settled in. Many rabbits escaped and found new homes in the fields and countryside.

TODAY

Rabbits are the third-most-popular pet in the world after cats and dogs. There are now more than 200 breeds worldwide.

VICTORIANS

Life changed for some rabbits in the 1800s. The Victorians could see rabbits had other charms besides being hunted and kept for food. It became fashionable to attend rabbit competitions, where owners would compete to see who had the best bunny. People also began to keep rabbits as pets for lucky boys and girls.

600 C.E.

1800s

1939

MONKS

From 600 C.E., there are records of rabbits being kept in **monasteries**, where monks lived and worked. Although the rabbits were still used for food and clothing, the monks took pride in caring for them and began to breed varieties with different coats and markings.

WORLD WAR II

During World War II (1939–1945), the British government encouraged people to keep rabbits to help feed families when food was limited. After the war ended, many people kept their rabbits as pets.

BUNNY STARS

There have been some legendary rabbits in books and on screen. How much do you know about these bunny superstars?

BUGS BUNNY

Everyone has heard of Bugs Bunny. The wisecracking rabbit has been around for nearly 90 years and has his own star on the Hollywood Walk of Fame. His first appearance was in a short cartoon that was nominated for an Oscar!

DID YOU KNOW?

Mel Blanc (the voice of Bugs Bunny) munched on real carrots while recording the character.

PETER RABBIT

When Beatrix Potter first wrote *The Tale of Peter Rabbit*, her publishers didn't think it would be much of a success. Today, the little book has sold more than 40 million copies and has been translated into more than 35 different languages! It has also been turned into a TV series and a popular movie.

THE WHITE RABBIT

If it weren't for this little bunny, Alice may never have fallen down the rabbit hole into Wonderland! Written in 1865 by Lewis Carroll, the book *Alice's Adventures in Wonderland* has made the White Rabbit almost as famous as the Mad Hatter or Alice herself.

DID YOU KNOW?

Alice's Adventures in Wonderland has been translated into 174 different languages!

MIFFY

This cute little white rabbit was created by Dutch artist Dick Bruna in the 1950s and is still popular today. Miffy has been featured in more than 30 books that have sold 85 million copies all over the world. She can be found on everything from pajamas to lunch boxes.

DID YOU KNOW?

Miffy's birthday is June 21 and she is more than 60 years old!

REMARKABLE RABBITS

These rabbits are the biggest, longest, and furriest bunnies around. Keep reading to discover their amazing achievements!

DID YOU KNOW?

The Flemish Giant rabbit is the largest domesticated rabbit breed. They can weigh up to 22 pounds (9.9 kg).

Nipper's Geronimo was an English Lop just like this one!

LONGEST EARS

An English Lop named Nipper's Geronimo had the longest ears of any rabbit. They measured 31 inches (79 cm) long!

OLD-TIMER

The oldest known rabbit lived to be 18 years and 10 months old. He was a wild rabbit caught in Tasmania, Australia, in 1964 and was named Flopsy.

GIANT BUNNY

Darius is a Flemish Giant rabbit, just like the one shown below. At 51 inches (129 cm), he has been recognized as the world's longest rabbit and is about the same size as a small dog. Although they look hard to handle, Flemish Giants are easy to look after because they are so relaxed!

MORE AMAZING BUNNY FACTS!

■ The longest recorded rabbit jump was made by Yabo, a rabbit from Denmark. Yabo's jump measured 9.84 feet (3 m) in length.

■ The highest rabbit jump ever recorded is 39.2 inches (99.5 cm) by a bunny named Mimrelunds Tosen, also from Denmark.

HAIR-RAISING RABBIT

Franchesca is a beautiful English Angora rabbit with record-breaking fur! At 14.37 inches (36.5 cm) long, it is the longest rabbit fur in the world, and Franchesca is often mistaken for a Pekingese dog!

Angora rabbits like this one need to be brushed regularly or their fur can get matted.

DID YOU KNOW?

Angora rabbits can make great pets. They are intelligent and love to play with their owners.

FIVE FACTS

Take a look at these amazing (and sometimes gross) facts about our wonderful bunny friends.

1 THEY EAT THEIR OWN POOP

It's weird, but true! Rabbits make two types of poop: soft black balls and hard pellets. By eating the soft poop, rabbits can get even more **nutrients** from their food.

2 THEY SLEEP WITH THEIR EYES OPEN

Rabbits can fall asleep while they are still on the lookout for predators.

3

THEY AREN'T RODENTS

Rabbits come from a family that also includes hares.

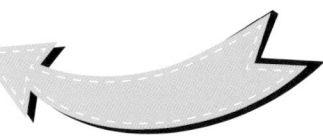

4

THEY CAN'T VOMIT

Rabbits don't have the ability to throw up, so it's vital that you feed them the right food to keep their stomachs healthy.

5

THEY ARE CREPUSCULAR

That is just a fancy way of saying rabbits are most active in the early morning and early evening.

YOUR BEST BUNNY

Can you match your personality to your dream pet?
Answer the questions and follow the arrows to find out!

HOW OFTEN WOULD YOU LIKE TO BRUSH YOUR PET?

Not very often

DO GOOD THINGS COME IN SMALL PACKAGES?

Definitely

Indoors

Not always

WOULD YOU KEEP YOUR RABBIT INDOORS OR OUTDOORS?

Outdoors

All the time

Playful

LET'S TALK EARS. FLOPPY OR STRAIGHT?

Straight

WOULD YOU LIKE YOUR PET TO BE CUTE OR PLAYFUL?

Cute

Floppy

WOULD YOUR PET BE BETTER AT SNUGGLING OR HOPPING?

Snuggling

MINI REX

The Mini Rex is a cute little bundle that likes a lot of attention. You and your bunny would be best friends and have so much fun together.

Hopping

Thumper

WHICH BUNNY DO YOU PREFER— PETER RABBIT OR THUMPER?

Peter

DUTCH RABBIT

Dutch rabbits are playful and happy bunnies, which is a great match for you! Give your bunny plenty of toys and attention and you'll be friends forever.

Yes

ARE YOU SPORTY?

No

Yes

HOLLAND LOP

If you don't mind a bit of brushing, the Holland Lop is your perfect match. With floppy ears and a stylish hairdo, this is the right rabbit for you!

DO YOU HAVE MANY OTHER PETS?

No

QUIZ!

Now that you've read all about rabbits, do you think you are a pet expert? Take this quiz to find out!

1 WHAT IS A FEMALE BUNNY CALLED?

a) a flo
b) a doe
c) a bow

2 HOW BIG IS A FULLY GROWN COLUMBIA BASIN PYGMY RABBIT?

a) the same size as a kitten
b) the same size as a fox
c) the same size as a mouse

3 HOW MANY TYPES OF POOP DO RABBITS MAKE?

a) one
b) two
c) three

4 HOW LONG ARE RABBITS PREGNANT FOR?

a) 30 days
b) 60 days
c) 90 days

The answers can be found on page 30.

5

WHY SHOULDN'T YOU KEEP RABBITS AND GUINEA PIGS IN THE SAME HOME?

a) they fight
b) they don't understand each other
c) both of the above

6

WHICH FOOD SHOULD RABBITS AVOID?

a) celery
b) clover
c) avocado

7

WHAT TYPE OF FLOOR IS HARMFUL TO BUNNIES?

a) marble
b) wire
c) wood

QUIZ ANSWERS

1. b   2. a   3. b   4. a   5. c   6. c   7. b   8. b   9. c   10. c

10

WHAT TYPE OF RABBIT HAS THE LONGEST FUR?

a) Flemish Giant
b) Dutch rabbit
c) Angora

9

WHO WROTE THE TALE OF PETER RABBIT?

a) J.K. Rowling
b) Eric Carle
c) Beatrix Potter

8

APPROXIMATELY HOW MANY BREEDS OF RABBITS ARE THERE WORLDWIDE?

a) 20
b) 200
c) 2000

GLOSSARY

anxious
Worried or nervous

breed
A group of animals that share the same characteristics and physical appearance

climate change
Earth becoming warmer as a result of pollution in the air, which has an effect on the environment

coat
An animal's fur

convulsions
A shaking movement of the body that cannot be controlled

domesticated
Living or working alongside humans

extinct
Describing an animal or plant that no longer exists

graze
To eat lightly throughout the day

heatstroke
An illness caused by being exposed to too much heat

hutch
A rabbit's home, usually made out of wood

lop
Drooping down instead of standing up straight

matting
Tangling into a thick lump

monasteries
Buildings kept for prayer, where monks or nuns live and work

nutrient
A natural substance that helps animals and plants grow

pregnant
Describing a rabbit with kittens growing inside her

run
An outdoor enclosure for a rabbit

toxic
Poisonous

vaccinate
To give medicine to a person or animal to stop them from becoming sick

vet
A medical doctor who treats animals; short for veterinarian

wean
To introduce food other than mother's milk to a baby rabbit

INDEX